First World War
and Army of Occupation
War Diary
France, Belgium and Germany

3 CAVALRY DIVISION
7 Cavalry Brigade
7 Machine Gun Squadron
29 February 1916 - 18 June 1919

WO95/1154/3

The Naval & Military Press Ltd
www.nmarchive.com
Published in association with The National Archives

Published by

The Naval & Military Press Ltd

Unit 10 Ridgewood Industrial Park,

Uckfield, East Sussex,

TN22 5QE England

Tel: +44 (0) 1825 749494

www.naval-military-press.com

www.nmarchive.com

This diary has been reprinted in facsimile from the original. Any imperfections are inevitably reproduced and the quality may fall short of modern type and cartographic standards.

© **Crown Copyright**
Images reproduced by permission of The National Archives, London, England, 2015.

Contents

Document type	Place/Title	Date From	Date To
Heading	WO95/1154/3 3 Cavalry Division 7 Cavalry Brigade 7 Machine Gun Squadron Feb 1916-June 1919		
Heading	1916-1919 3 rd Cavalry Division 7th Cavalry Brigade. 7th Machine Gun Squadron Feb 1916-Jun 1919		
Heading	7 Bde M G Sqd Vol I II & III 29.2.16 to 30.4.16		
War Diary	Hucqueliers	29/02/1916	04/05/1916
War Diary	Alx-en-Ergny	13/05/1916	13/05/1916
War Diary	Wambercourt	15/05/1916	15/05/1916
War Diary	Le Plessiel	16/05/1916	21/05/1916
War Diary	Wambercourt	22/05/1916	22/05/1916
War Diary	Alx-en-Ergny	25/05/1916	30/05/1916
War Diary	Merlimont Plage	01/06/1916	06/06/1916
War Diary	Alx-en-Ergny	07/06/1916	24/06/1916
War Diary	Crecy	24/06/1916	24/06/1916
War Diary	Bethencourt Les Dames	25/06/1916	25/06/1916
War Diary	Corbie	26/06/1916	04/07/1916
War Diary	Wanel	04/07/1916	04/07/1916
War Diary	Corbie	08/07/1916	01/08/1916
War Diary	Oissy	02/08/1916	02/08/1916
War Diary	St Riquier	04/08/1916	04/08/1916
War Diary	Dominois	05/08/1916	05/08/1916
War Diary	Aix En Ergny	14/08/1916	10/09/1916
War Diary	Grandpreaux	11/09/1916	11/09/1916
War Diary	Domvast	12/09/1916	12/09/1916
War Diary	Bourdon	13/09/1916	14/09/1916
War Diary	Bussy Les Daours.	15/09/1916	15/09/1916
War Diary	Bonnay.	16/09/1916	17/09/1916
War Diary	Querrieu	18/09/1916	21/09/1916
War Diary	Hangest	22/09/1916	22/09/1916
War Diary	Boffles	23/09/1916	23/09/1916
War Diary	Loison Sur Crequoise	24/09/1916	20/10/1916
War Diary	Crequy	21/10/1916	07/02/1917
War Diary	Bois Tean	12/02/1917	26/02/1917
War Diary	Bois Tean	04/03/1917	29/03/1917
War Diary	Bearainville	06/04/1917	10/04/1917
War Diary	Tilloy.	11/04/1917	12/04/1917
War Diary	Berneville	13/04/1917	16/04/1917
War Diary	Willencourt.	19/04/1917	19/04/1917
War Diary	Raye-Sur-Authie	20/04/1917	15/05/1917
War Diary	Fouilloy	17/05/1917	17/05/1917
War Diary	Ceresy	19/05/1917	19/05/1917
War Diary	Tincourt	20/05/1917	03/07/1917
War Diary	Suzanne	05/07/1917	05/07/1917
War Diary	Buire-S-B	06/07/1917	06/07/1917
War Diary	Etree-Wamin	08/07/1917	08/07/1917
War Diary	Vandelicourt	10/07/1917	31/07/1917
War Diary	Guarbecqe	09/08/1917	31/08/1917
War Diary	Bours.	07/09/1917	27/10/1917
War Diary	Domqueur	01/11/1917	16/11/1917
War Diary	St. Gratien	17/11/1917	17/11/1917

War Diary	Proyart.	18/11/1917	22/11/1917
War Diary	Beacourt.	23/11/1917	30/11/1917
War Diary	Beaucourt Sur L'Hallue	01/12/1917	01/12/1917
War Diary	Trenches	09/12/1917	22/12/1917
War Diary	Berneuil	22/12/1917	31/01/1918
War Diary	W. 3 C.S. 7	01/02/1918	28/02/1918
War Diary	Trefcon	03/03/1918	09/03/1918
War Diary	Wiencourt	10/03/1918	10/03/1918
War Diary	Briquemesnuil	11/03/1918	11/03/1918
War Diary	Fontaine	12/03/1918	12/03/1918
War Diary	Epagne.	13/03/1918	25/03/1918
War Diary	Arras. (Fauberg St Sauveur)	25/03/1918	29/03/1918
Heading	7th Cav. Bde. 3rd Cav. Div. War Diary 7th Machine Gun Squadron. April (1st to 14th) 1918		
Miscellaneous	Officer 1/e Records Cavalry Records Base.		
War Diary	Wagnonlieu	01/04/1918	11/04/1918
War Diary	Ramecourt	12/04/1918	12/04/1918
War Diary	Contes.	13/04/1918	13/04/1918
War Diary	Etaples.	14/04/1918	14/04/1918
War Diary	Fiefs	01/05/1918	04/05/1918
War Diary	Linzeux	05/05/1918	05/05/1918
War Diary	Maizicourt	06/05/1918	06/05/1918
War Diary	Contay	07/05/1918	17/05/1918
War Diary	St. Ouen	19/05/1918	24/05/1918
War Diary	Montigny	25/05/1918	31/05/1918
War Diary	Belloy-Sur-Somme	31/05/1918	14/06/1918
War Diary	Montigny	15/06/1918	22/06/1918
War Diary	St. Ouen	23/06/1918	06/08/1918
War Diary	Bourdon	06/08/1918	14/08/1918
Heading	W. of Dommartin	15/08/1918	15/08/1918
War Diary	St. Ouen	16/08/1918	25/08/1918
War Diary	Le Boisle Canchy	25/08/1918	31/08/1918
War Diary	Fillievres	06/09/1918	10/09/1918
War Diary	Rougefay	12/09/1918	16/09/1918
War Diary	Blingel	17/09/1918	17/09/1918
War Diary	Heuzecourt	18/09/1918	18/09/1918
War Diary	Rougefay	19/09/1918	19/09/1918
War Diary	Galametz	25/09/1918	25/09/1918
War Diary	Terramesnil	26/09/1918	26/09/1918
War Diary	Aveluy	27/09/1918	27/09/1918
War Diary	Hem	28/09/1918	29/09/1918
War Diary	Vermand	30/09/1918	03/10/1918
War Diary	Bellenglise	03/10/1918	03/10/1918
War Diary	Magny-La-Fosse	03/10/1918	03/10/1918
War Diary	Vermand	04/10/1918	08/10/1918
War Diary	Joncourt	08/10/1918	08/10/1918
War Diary	Geneve	08/10/1918	08/10/1918
War Diary	Etricourt	09/10/1918	09/10/1918
War Diary	Geneve	09/10/1918	09/10/1918
War Diary	Maretz	09/10/1918	09/10/1918
War Diary	Reumont	09/10/1918	10/10/1918
War Diary	Le Cateau	10/10/1918	10/10/1918
War Diary	Troisville	10/10/1918	10/10/1918
War Diary	Bertry	11/10/1918	13/10/1918
War Diary	Honnecourt	14/10/1918	14/10/1918
War Diary	Neuville-Bourjonval	17/10/1918	31/10/1918

War Diary	Nuville	01/11/1918	08/11/1918
War Diary	Tourcoing	09/11/1918	18/11/1918
War Diary	Groote-Hearding	21/11/1918	21/11/1918
War Diary	Dongleberg	22/11/1918	30/11/1918
War Diary	Fumal	15/12/1918	15/12/1918
War Diary	Nandrin	16/12/1918	26/12/1918
War Diary	Mean.	27/12/1918	27/12/1918
War Diary	Chateau-Bassine Mean Maffe Bonsin Borlon area	01/01/1919	08/03/1919
War Diary	Hermalle Sous Huy.	15/03/1919	30/04/1919
War Diary	Basse-Awirs. (Near Engis)	01/05/1919	31/05/1919
Miscellaneous	Officer E/c a.G's Office, H Q British Troops in France & Flanders	18/06/1919	18/16/1919
War Diary	Basses-Awirs Near (Engis)	01/06/1919	18/06/1919

(3)

WO 95/1154

3 Cavalry Division

7 Cavalry Brigade

7 Machine Gun Squadron

Feb 1916 – June 1919

1916-1919
3RD CAVALRY DIVISION
7TH CAVALRY BRIGADE.

7TH MACHINE GUN SQUADRON
FEB 1916 - JUN 1919

3c

4 Rue M.G. Sqa

Vol I II & III

29.2.16 to 30.4.16.

Formed 29.2.16.
to
June 1918.

Army Form C. 2118

WAR DIARY
or
INTELLIGENCE SUMMARY

7th Machine Gun Squadron.

(Erase heading not required.)

Instructions regarding War Diaries and Intelligence Summaries are contained in F.S. Regs., Part II and the Staff Manual respectively. Title Pages will be prepared in manuscript.

Place	Date	Hour	Summary of Events and Information	Remarks and references to Appendices
HUCQUELIERS	29/2/16		Squadron was formed. Section No 1 and 2 from 1st Life Guards. Section No 3 and 4 from 2nd Life Guards. Sections Nos 5 and 6 from Leicestershire Yeomanry. The following came in at strength. Major A.M. PIRIE. D.S.O. 21st Lancers att. 1st Life Guards Command. No 1 Section Lieut C.D. LEYLAND 1st Life Guards, No 2 Section 2/Lieut C.R.L. ENGLISH 1st Life Guards. No 3 Section Lieut F.N. GRIFFIN 2nd Life Guards No 4 Section Lieut T. PHILIPSON 2nd Life Guards No 5 Section 2/Lieut C.R. MARSH Leicestershire Yeomanry No 6 Section 2/Lieut B.B. GRIFFIN Leicestershire Yeomanry.	
	14/3/16		Sections known as their Regimental Nos till tue 14/3/16. Nos 1 and 2 Sections moved from Hucls. at RUMILLY to new billets at HUCQUELIERS. Nos 5 and 6 Sections to new billets at AVESNES. WICQUINGHEM	
	8/4/16		No 3057 Pte WARD.C. Leicestershire Yeomanry accidently wounded and died of wounds same day	
	18/4/16		2/Lieut N.S. ROUSE 2nd Life Guards (since attached) and took over No 4 Section. Lt. T. PHILIPSON No 3 Section Lt. F.N. GRIFFIN taking over duties as Senior in Command.	
	19/4/16 30/4/16		Squadron remains in same billets working chiefly in Cavalry Training	

WAR DIARY
~~INTELLIGENCE SUMMARY~~

Army Form C. 2118

7 M. Gun Sqd
Vol 4

Place	Date	Hour	Summary of Events and Information	Remarks and references to Appendices
HUCQUELIERS	1/5/16		Squadron remained in billets.	
	4/5/16			
AIX-EN-ERGNY			The squadron changed billets to AIX-EN-ERGNY. Horses being picketted in its open.	
"	13/5/16		Brigade marched to FRESSIN – CONTES area marching independently by Squadrons. Billeted in WAMBERCOURT sharing commune with 'K' Ritta.	
WAMBERCOURT	15/5/16		Brigade continued march to training ground near ST RIQUIER. Squadron left billets at 6.30 a.m. watering at 9.30 a.m. & reached or LE PLESSIEL at 12-45 p.m.	
LE PLESSIEL	16/5/16		Training ground was at disposal of the Brigade from 10 a.m. to 2 p.m. Sections were at disposal of their leaders to practise jumping & extn -	
	17/5/16		Training ground at disposal of Brigade from 6 a.m. till 10 a.m.	
	18/5/16		Divisional day with G.O.C. Reserve Corps	
	19/5/16		Training (mounted) at disposal of Brigade from 11 a.m. to 7.30 p.m.	
	20/5/16		Divisional day under G.O.C. 6th Cav. Brigade	
	21/5/16		Return march commenced. Squadron marched independently at 7 a.m. to WAMBERCOURT	
WAMBERCOURT	22/5/16		Squadron marched at 4 a.m. to AIX-EN-ERGNY arriving at 7 a.m.	
AIX-EN-ERGNY	24/5/16		No. 3 and 4 Sections under Lt. PHILIPSON marched at 4.30 in company with 2nd Life Guards to MERLIMONT for training –	
	30/5/16		Remainder of Squadron marched at 6 a.m. to MERLIMONT PLAGE arriving 11-30 a.m. No. 3 & 4 Sections rejoining the Squadron.	

J.P.Griffiths

WAR DIARY
or
INTELLIGENCE SUMMARY

(Erase heading not required.)

Army Form C. 2118

7th Green Sgt VR 5

Place	Date	Hour	Summary of Events and Information	Remarks and references to Appendices
MERLIMONT PLAGE	1.6.16 6.6.16		Squadron remained at MERLIMONT PLAGE training & carrying out target practice	
AIX-EN-ERGNY	7.6.16 24.6.16		Squadron marched back to billets at AIX-EN-ERGNY	
CRECY	24.6.16		The squadron marched at 4.30pm to the brigade rendezvous at HENONVILLE, & moved with the brigade to CRECY arriving there at 12.30am, bivouaced in a field close to the town. The following officers marched with the squadron: Major A.M. PIRIE DSO Lt. C. LEYLAND Lt. T. PHILIPSON 2nd Lt. C.A. MARSH " N.S. TOUSE " C.R.L. ENGLISH " B.B. GRIFFIN.	
BETHENCOURT LES DAMES	25.6.16		Brigade left CRECY at 7.30pm & arrived at BETHENCOURT LES DAMES at 8am.	
CORBIE	26.6.16		Brigade left BETHENCOURT-LES-DAMES at 5pm, arrived at CORBIE at 11am.	
CORBIE	26.6.16 30.6.16		Brigade remained at CORBIE.	

Army Form C. 2118

WAR DIARY
or
INTELLIGENCE SUMMARY
(Erase heading not required.)

7th Machine Gun Squadron — Vol 6

Place	Date	Hour	Summary of Events and Information	Remarks and references to Appendices
CORBIE	1.7.16 to 4.7.16		Squadron remained at CORBIE standing to at one hours notice to move.	
WANEL	4.7.16		Squadron marched 35 miles to WANEL near ABBEVILLE, leaving at 6am & arriving 6.30pm. Lt F.N.GRIFFIN rejoined the Squadron.	
CORBIE	8.7.16 to 30/7/16		Squadron marched at 1 p.m. to CORBIE arriving 10 p.m. and bivouaced on the bank of the Somme. Squadron remained at CORBIE standing to at varying degrees of Readiness.	

Army Form C. 2118

WAR DIARY or INTELLIGENCE SUMMARY
(Erase heading not required.)

Mth. M.G.Sq
Mth. M.G.Sq.

Place	Date	Hour	Summary of Events and Information	Remarks and references to Appendices
CORBIE	1/8/16		Squadron marched at 9am. to DISSY arriving 12 noon - at 3pm. 2/Lt MARSH proceeded with advance party from Reserve army to reconnoitre trenches in the ZEIPSIG REDOUBT Salient -	
DISSY	2/8/16		Squadron less 2 Section (chinwounks) marched at 4am. to ST RIQUIER - 2/Lt ENGLISH with Nº 2 and 5 gun team (29 OR) proceeded at 7-30am. by bus to join 2/Lt MARSH	
ST-RIQUIER	4/8/16		Squadron marched at 6am. to DOMINOIS arriving 11am. Major A.M. PIRIE D.S.O. proceeded under W.O. orders to England and Lt. S.G.F. CROMLEY 1st K.E. assumed Command.	
DOMINOIS	5/8/16		Squadron marched at 9am. to Mri-en-ERGNY arriving 11-30am. and went into permanent billets -	
Mri-en-ERGNY	14/8/16 to 16/8/16		Nº 2 and 5 Sections returned from trenches having suffered casualties 3 wounded. Lt. C.S. KERNICK and for attachment from W.L. Corps Base depot.	
"	23/8/16 to 24/8/16		Mounted training and tactical exercises 2/Lt C.K. MARSH proceeded under W.O. instructions to ENGLAND & Lt. C.S. KERNICK and 25 OR proceeded 4 bus to BUZINCOURT this mounted party -	
"	29/8/16		Lt. F.M. GRIFFIN evacuated to hospital.	
"	to 31/8/16		Squadron training.	

Army Form C. 2118

WAR DIARY
or
INTELLIGENCE SUMMARY
(Erase heading not required.)

To machine gun Squadron

Place	Date	Hour	Summary of Events and Information	Remarks and references to Appendices
AIX EN ERGNY	7.9.16.		2/Lt C.S. KERNICK and 2.8.O.R. returned by motor bus from BUZINCOURT	
"	10.9.16.		Squadron left billets at 8.45 a.m. and marched with 1st LIFE GUARDS & "K" Battery under the command of Lt Col E.H. BRASSEY M.V.O. to GRAND TREAUX where the Squadron billeted for the night.	
GRANDTREAUX	11.9.16		Squadron marched at 1.30 p.m. with 2nd LIFE GUARDS under Lt Col Hon. A. STANLEY D.S.O. to DOMVAST. arriving at 6 p.m.	
DOMVAST	12.9.16.		Squadron marched as a unit in the brigade. Rendezvous Y Roads 1½ miles N of St RICQUIER at 10 a.m. Arriving at BOURDON at 3 p.m. The following officers marched from permanent billets with the Sqdn. Capt. O.S.L. CHORLEY Lt C.D. LEYLAND. 2Lt T. PHILIPSON. 2Lt N.S. ROUSE. 2Lt C.R.L. ENGLISH. 2Lt B.B. GRIFFIN 2Lt C.S. KERNICK.	
BOURDON	13.9.16		Remained in Bivouack at BOURDON.	
"	14 " "		Brigade marched at 8 a.m. to BUSSY LES DAOURS. arriving at 3 p.m. Took over area evacuated that morning by the 3rd Indian Division. Three sleeping & ration huts erected in the evening.	
BUSSY LES DAOURS	15 " "		Squadron paraded at 7 a.m. marched with the brigade to afternoon of reviews at BONNAY. arrived there about 9 a.m. & from 11 a.m. started to attend at & hour intervals. B. echelon was left behind under Major Crawley L.V.C. at BUSSY - At 7.30 p.m. the squadron moved into an adjoining field bivouacked for the night.	
BONNAY.	16 " "		Squadron was at ½ hours notice from 8 a.m. Orders received at 1.30 a.m. that the brigade was to move to new area at QUERRIEU. This area was necessary to make room for the 2nd Cav. Div. who	
"	17 " "		were moving back on account of the shortage of water.	

WAR DIARY
or
INTELLIGENCE SUMMARY
(Erase heading not required.)

Army Form C. 2118

Place	Date	Hour	Summary of Events and Information	Remarks and references to Appendices
QUERRIEU	18th		Squadron remained in bivouack. Poured with rain all day. Lieut. Hon. M.H. PELHAM 1st LIFE GUARDS joined the Squadron from England & took on No.1 section.	
"	21st		Brigade marched to a billeting area W. of AMIENS. Squadron billets at HANGEST.	
HANGEST	22nd		Paraded 9 a.m. and marched to BOFFLES.	
BOFFLES	23rd		Paraded 8.15 a.m. and marched to LOISON SUR CREQUOISE	
LOISON SUR CREQUOISE	24th - 30th		Unable to do mounted training owing to bad weather.	

1875 Wt. W593/826 1,000,000 4/15 J.B.C. & A. A.D.S.S./Forms/C. 2118.

Army Form C. 2118

WAR DIARY
or
INTELLIGENCE SUMMARY 7A. M. Gun Sqn.
(Erase heading not required.)

Vol 9

Place	Date	Hour	Summary of Events and Information	Remarks and references to Appendices
LOISON SUR CREQUOISE	Oct 15th		LEICESTERSHIRE YEOMANRY double section transferred to 8th Machine Gun Squadron. 2/Lt. B.B. GRIFFIN & 2/Lt W.G. WHATFIELD.	
	Oct 20th		ROYAL HORSE GUARDS double section transferred from 8th Machine Gun Squadron to 7th Squadron. Lt. D.R. TREFUSIS & 2/Lt H.W. DALTON (M.G.C)	
	" 21st		The Squadron hired out horse kitchen from LOISON to CREQUY. Lt. D.R. TREFUSIS (R.H.G) proceeded to M.G.C depot at VERFIELD to instruct.	
CREQUY	" 22nd		2/Lt T. BRYCE-WILSON (Car. Res) M.G. Corps joined vice Lt TREFUSIS to England.	
"	23rd 30th }		Improving horse-standings clipping horses.	

WAR DIARY or INTELLIGENCE SUMMARY

Army Form C. 2118

Vol 10

Place	Date	Hour	Summary of Events and Information	Remarks and references to Appendices
CREQUY	1-27 Mar.			
	6.10.16		Clipping horses and working at improvement of billets	
	12/11/16		2 ORs attached from RE's for repair of stables	
	13/11/16		L/Corp. MILLS I.L.G. attended 5 days course at anti-gas school. Lieut. J.H. YARNALL sent by O.C. 1st L.G. Completed Course of Instruction in bayonet fighting to 6 NCOs	
	24/11/16		Lieut H.M.H. PELHAM attended 3 days course at anti-gas school	
	25/11/16		1 NCO and 16 men sent to RE 3rd Field Squadron	
	26/11/16		Capt. GUY R.H.G. attended 5 days course at anti gas School	
	26/11/16		Classes in bayonet fighting and M.G. Mechanism commenced.	
	29/11/16		Armourer S.S. WHATELEY. A.O.D. sent to Workshops MONTREUIL on one months course.	
	29/11/16		2 auxiliary horse wagons G.S. with teams and drivers attached to Squadron	
	30/11/16		Lieut C.D. LEYLAND. Sent to M.G. Training Centre UCKFIELD to replace Lieut J.R. TREFUSIS.	

WAR DIARY or INTELLIGENCE SUMMARY

Army Form C. 2118

7th M.G. Sqn. Vol XI

Place	Date	Hour	Summary of Events and Information	Remarks and references to Appendices
CREAUX	Dec. 1.		Clipping horses and working at improvement of billets.	
	2.12.16.		Lce. Cpl. OLIVER sent to M.G. training centre, UCKFIELD.	
	6.12.16.		2nd Lt. H.W. DALTON sent on a 3 days course at Anti gas school at WAILLY.	
	9.12.16.		I.O.R. sent to Divisional cookery school at St POL.	
	11.12.16.		Lce. Cpl. WORMAN, 2.I.C.G. sent on a 5 days course at gas school at WAILLY.	
	15.12.16.		17 O.R's sent to 2/9 Field Squadron R.E. returned.	
	22.12.16.		Lce. Cpl. CARTER, 2.I.C. and Lce Cpl. CORNER, 1.I.G. returned from M.G. training centre UCKFIELD.	
	20.12.16.		LIEUT. T. PHILIPSON sent on 3 days course at gas school, WAILLY.	
	22.12.16.		Marching order Parade in preparation for g.o.c's inspection.	
	23.12.16.		g.o.c.b inspected squadron in marching order.	
	26.12.16.		Leave stopped and squadron's allotment of leave given to 8th Brigade.	
	26.12.16.		Capt. CROMBIE went on a 3 weeks advanced M.G. course at CAMIERS. LIEUT. T. PHILIPSON assumed command of squadron during his absence.	
	27.12.16.		C.Q.M.S HAYDON sent on 5 days course at gas school, WAILLY.	
	28.12.16.		Armourer S.S. WHATELEY A.O.D returned from course in the workshops at MONTREUIL.	

WAR DIARY
or
INTELLIGENCE SUMMARY

Army Form C. 2118

7 M G Squd
Vol XI

Place	Date	Hour	Summary of Events and Information	Remarks and references to Appendices
CREQUY	3/1/17		Lt O R Trefusis returned from WERFIELD	
	6/1/17		Lt ROUSE attended Gas Course at WAILLY	
	10/1/17		Capt Chomley returned from CAMIERS	
	11/1/17		Interpreter Asst Lieut R Soyer transferred to S'Bde	
	12/1/17		5 officers (Capt Chomley, Lieut Philipson, Lt-m McLean, Group Ht, Lt T B Wilson, 91 O.R's were left in case of B.y.y. Gregory on 17th Jan. until Cdn Inf Bde. former 23 Got dug in night of 10th and 3rd Canadian Inf Bde. at VIMY RIDGE 4 guns met each of 10th and 3rd Canadian Inf Bde. Hq at VILLERS au BOIS	
	22/1/17		Sgt Inglish left for MG course L CAMIERS	
	23/1/17		L/cpl A H Hall L.G. went for MG course L CAMIERS	
	23/1/17		L/cpl Couret L.G. went on Gas course	
	30/1/17		General party relieved in 4 Canadian Division area by spare party of 6th M.G.S. 7 M.G.S. spares returned by motor lorry L CREQUY	
			Spares suffered no casualties from wounds or sickness	
	31/1/17		Lt T.B. Wilson went to Gas course at WAILLY	
	31/1/17		Clearing up billets preparatory to leaving for VERTON on 1st Feb	

CREQUY.

Army Form C. 2118

WAR DIARY
or
INTELLIGENCE SUMMARY

(Erase heading not required.)

7th M. Gun Sqn.

Vol/13

Instructions regarding War Diaries and Intelligence Summaries are contained in F.S. Regs., Part II. and the Staff Manual respectively. Title Pages will be prepared in manuscript.

Place	Date	Hour	Summary of Events and Information	Remarks and references to Appendices
CREQUY	1/2/17		Squadron went from CREQUY to VERTON.	
	2/2/17 to 7/2/17		Capt C.D. LEYLAND rejoined from VERFIELD. VERTON.	
	3/2/17		Troops Cook to Rouen (cookery school).	
	7/2/17		Squadron moved from VERTON to BOIS JEAN. 1 section at BAHOT 1 Section EBRUYERES. 1 section AIGUILLE.	
BOIS JEAN	19/2/17		6 inch having commenced (after absence proper).	
	20/2/17		1 G.S. wagon returned Q.M.T. Co., 1 R.A.M.C. wagon also taken att. No 1 section from 7th C.F.A	
	16/2/17 26/2/17		San Conver { Lt D.R. TREVOR Capt G.G.F. CHOMLEY	

WAR DIARY or INTELLIGENCE SUMMARY

7 M G Sqdn

Army Form C. 2118

Place	Date	Hour	Summary of Events and Information	Remarks and references to Appendices
BOIS JEAN	14th and 15th March		Squadron Training	
	14th March		Lt Philipson & L/Cpl Hon M Pelham returned from Gunnery School.	
	15"		7 ORs received as reinforcement.	
	16th		Capt Vrooten R.H.Q. to Achiet	
	17th		Major Church on leave from 17th to 27th. Capt Leyland in Command.	
	19th		L/Cpt Heeds 2 I.C. went to M.G. Course COYIERS	
	22nd		Nuclear R.W.C. MSSM 2 men and 2 horses returned to 7 C.F.A.	
	24th		2/Lt J B Wilson & thirteen 1st C.R. English returned from Harbour	
	24th		Capt. Ligne & England to Command.	
	25th		Two men sent on Pigeon Course	
	28th		G.O.C. inspection at Moreuil. L/Cpt Heer from Hehkles	
	29th		Squadron fitted unit for rehersal at RANG DU FLIERS	

Army Form C. 2118.

7th Machine Gun Squadron

APRIL 1917

WAR DIARY
or
INTELLIGENCE SUMMARY.
(Erase heading not required.)

Place	Date	Hour	Summary of Events and Information	Remarks and references to Appendices
BOIS JEAN	April 4th		Squadron training.	
"	" 5th		Squadron marched to BEURAINVILLE. The following officers marched with the Squadron. Major. G.G.F. CHOMLEY. CAPT. C.D.LEYLAND. 2nd LT. T. PHILLIPSON. D.R. TRETUSIS. Hon M.H. PELHAM. N.S. ROUSE. CR.L. ENGLISH. 2/Lt H.W. DALTON. Dismounted body marches ½ hr C.S. KERNICK by tram to BEAURAINVILLE.	
BEAURAINVILLE	6th		Remained in billets.	
	7th		To BOUBERS-SUR-CANCHE.	
	8th		Squadron paraded at 2pm. marched with the brigade to GOUY-EN-ARTOIS 'B' echelon remained at BOUBERS-SUR-CANCHE.	
	9th		Brigade marched at 11.15 am. to ARRAS. Spent the night in afield 1 mile W. of ARRAS. Snow on the ground. Frost all night.	
	10th		Brigade marched at 8.30 pm. Turned out again during the night. 4 TILLOY 7.30 pm. Snowing hard. Frogs again during the night.	
TILLOY	11th		"Stand-to" at 5am. off saddled at 8am. at 4.30pm. brigade moved back to RACE COURSE W of ARRAS. Billeted cold night with snow falling. 'A' echelon rejoined the squadron at 8.30 pm.	

T2134. Wt. W708—776. 500000. 4/15. Sir J. C. & S.

Army Form C. 2118.

WAR DIARY
or
INTELLIGENCE SUMMARY.
(Erase heading not required.)

Place	Date	Hour	Summary of Events and Information	Remarks and references to Appendices
	April 12th		Brigade turned out at 5 a.m. to Gouy-en-Artois. Ordered afterwards operation. Left at 3.30 p.m. to billet in BERNEVILLE. Horses and men each under cover. "B" echelon reported the operation.	
BERNEVILLE	13.4.15		Remained in billets.	
"	16th		Orders received at 2.30 a.m. That Brigade would move to new billeting area. 7th M.G.S. to LANNOY. WILLENCOURT. LA NEUVILLE. Wavelin road off at 6.45 a.m.	
WILLENCOURT.	19th		Liaison board at G.H.S. a.m. to fresh billets at RAYE-SUR-AUTHIE. No. 6 Section to FOND DE VAL.	
RAYE-SUR-AUTHIE	20th		Dismounted Sundry approved operation.	
	26th		Horse inspection by G.O.C. Division arrange practice.	

WAR DIARY or INTELLIGENCE SUMMARY

Army Form C. 2118.

7th M.G. Sqdn.

May 1917

Place	Date	Hour	Summary of Events and Information	Remarks and references to Appendices
RAYE-SUR-AUTHIE	May 2nd		45 ORs received as reinforcements. M.G.C. Personnel returned to Base.	
"	8th		13 ORs reinforcement. M.G.C. Oddlss returned to Base.	
"	12th		Squadron marched from RAYE-S-AUTHIE to WILLENCOURT. The following Officers marched with the Squadron.. Maj: G.G.F. CHOMLEY. Capt. C.D. LEYLAND. Lts T. THILITSON. D.R. TREFUSIS. N.S. ROUSE. C.R.L. ENGLISH. 2/Lts H. W. DALTON. C.S. KERWICK. Lt Hon M.H. PELMAN to England on Leave.	
	13th		WILLENCOURT to BRETEL.	
	14th		BRETEL to VILLERS-BOCAGE.	
	15th		VILLERS-BOCAGE to FOUILLOY.	
FOUILLOY	17th		FOUILLOY to CERESY.	
CERESY	19th		CERESY to GROMACK near TINCOURT.	
TINCOURT	20th		2/Lts H.W. DALTON and C.S. KERWICK transferred to 13th with M.G. Sqdns respectively.	
"	22nd		No 1930 Cpl GOLDS R.H. Sch to England for a commission. Party left for the trenches — 4 Officers 110 ORs. Capt. C.D. LEYLAND Lts T. THILITSON. D.R. TREFUSIS. C.R. ENGLISH. Lt N.S. ROUSE returned.	
"	23rd			

Army Form C. 2118.

WAR DIARY
or
INTELLIGENCE SUMMARY.
(Erase heading not required.)

Instructions regarding War Diaries and Intelligence Summaries are contained in F.S. Regs., Part II. and the Staff Manual respectively. Title pages will be prepared in manuscript.

Place	Date	Hour	Summary of Events and Information	Remarks and references to Appendices
TINCOURT	23		in charge of permanent bivouac. The Squadron took on from the S.R.M.G. Sqdn in D2 Sectr.	
			13 ORs received as reinforcements. 13 ORs transferred to 1st LIFE GUARDS on authority of A.G. Base.	
	28.		Lt. Hon. M.H. PELHAM rejoined from leave. 2/Lt. E LE M. TRAFFORD and H.C.L. HAWTHORN as reinforcements.	
	29.		Lt. Hon. M.H. PELHAM joined Trench party.	
	31st		Trench party. All quiet and no Casualties to date.	

Army Form C. 2118.

WAR DIARY
or
INTELLIGENCE SUMMARY.
(Erase heading not required.)

7th M.G. Sqdn

Vol 17

Place	Date	Hour	Summary of Events and Information	Remarks and references to Appendices
	JUNE			
TINCOURT	5		Major GG Howsey took over Command of Squadron in relieves in Capt C S Leyland	
	7		Capt C S Leyland & Lieut Mills went to CAMIERS M.G. School to attend Machine Gun Course	
	11		Squadron in trenches relieved by 6th M.G.S	
	12.17		Squadron resting and refitting	
	20		Squadron relieved Major Clowrey relieved 8th M.G.S. in D1 Section front	
	21		3 O.R. returned by steel Frig. in BIRDCAGE (D1 Sector)	
	23		2 O.R. wounded by steel Frig. in Steen intruded line D2 Sector	
	29th		Squadron relieved in trenches by 3rd regt M.G.S.	
	30th		Capt C S Leyland & Lt/Off Mills returned from M.G.S. CAMIERS	

WAR DIARY or INTELLIGENCE SUMMARY

Army Form C. 2118.

7th MACHINE GUN SQUADRON

July 1917

Place	Date	Hour	Summary of Events and Information	Remarks and references to Appendices
TINCOURT	July 3	9.30am	Marched with Brigade to SUZANNE	
SUZANNE	5		" " " " BUIRE-SOUS-CORBIE	
BUIRE-S-B	6		" " " " ETREE-WAMIN	
ETREE-WAMIN	8		" " " " ~~AUGUST~~ VANDELICOURT	
VANDELICOURT	10		LIEUT N.S. ROUSE went to ENGLAND on one months leave	
"	10		2/LIEUT D.B. CHAPPLE joined the Squadron Supernumerary to Establishment	
"	8		TROOPERS CLARK & SPEIGHT attached 4 days LEWIS Gun Course at 1st Corps School	
"	"		TROOPERS COLTHART & PRIDEAUX " " " " at 1st Corps School	
"	10		LIEUT CPL ENGLISH attended 2 days LEWIS Gun Course at 6th M.G.S.	
"	16	5.2pm	Marched to AUCHEL	
"	17	5.15am	Marched to RUE DE QUARBECQUE	
"	27		Held Squadron Horse Show	
"	31		LIEUT T. PHILIPS OM went to ENGLAND on 10 days leave	
"	28		Corpl OWEN left for M.G. Course at G.H.Q. School CAMIERS	

WAR DIARY
~~INTELLIGENCE~~ SUMMARY
(Erase heading not required.)

7th Machine Gun Squadron   August 1917

Army Form C. 2118.

Place	Date	Hour	Summary of Events and Information	Remarks and references to Appendices
	1917.			
GOUARBECQUE	Aug 9th		Lieut ROUSE returned from 1 month's leave in England. Lieut PHILIPSON returned from 10 days leave in England.	
	Aug 12th		Lieut TREFUSIS went on 10 days leave in England.	
	Aug 17th		No 3003 Tpr. THOMPSON was accidentally shot by Cpl HEIGHTON. Consequent on the increase in establishment of N.C.O's the following promotions were made. 2086 Cpl WILLIS. 1st L.G. to be a/Sgt. 2617 Cpl HAYDON 1st L.G. to be a/Sgt. 2704 a/Cpl MARTEN 2nd L.G. to be a/Sgt. 1993 a/Cpl PRIOR R.H.G. to be a/Cpl of L.G. 3020 L/Cpl HEIGHTON. 1st L.G. to be a/Cpl. 2894 L/Cpl MARKWICK 1st L.G. to be a/Cpl. 3035 L/Cpl OLIVER. 1st L.G. to be a/Cpl. 3134 Lce/Cpl DORRIAN. 1st L.G. to be a/Cpl. 2823 Lce/Cpl NEEDS. 2nd L.G. to be a/Cpl. 1733 Lce/Cpl BARNSLEY R.H.G. to be a/Cpl. 2300 Lce/Cpl KING R.H.G. to be a/Cpl. 2350 La/Cpl YOUNG. 2nd L.G. to be a/Cpl. Cpl HEIGHTON 'reprimanded by Court of Enquiry.'	
	Aug 19th		Lieut. TREFUSIS returned from 10 days leave in England.	
	Aug 24th		Capt. LEYLAND went on 10 days leave to England.	
	Aug 25th		Lieut ENGELSEN. went on 10 days leave to England.	
	Aug 28th			
	Aug 31st		Major CHOMLEY went to CAMIERS for 1 month. Cpl A. MOSS went to CAMIERS for 1 month. Lieut PHILIPSON in command.	

Army Form C. 2118.

WAR DIARY
INTELLIGENCE SUMMARY.
(Erase heading not required.)

7th Machine Gun Squadron September

Place	Date	Hour	Summary of Events and Information	Remarks and references to Appendices
	Sept 1917.			
BOURS.	7th		Capt LEYLAND returned from 10 days leave in England.	
	8th		Lieut ENGLISH returned from 10 days leave in England.	
	10th		Tpr. NORRIS committed suicide. Finding of the court of enquiry was "Suicide whilst temporarily insane".	
	14th		Nº 1 & 2 subsections took part in a scheme with the First Life Guards.	
	16th		Tpr. CHINERY went on a course to the Third Army Cookery School at AIRE.	
	17th		Squadron transport inspected by D.A.D.S.C.	
	19th		Nos 3 & 4 subsections took part in a scheme with the Second Life Guards.	
	21st		Nº 5 & 6 subsections took part in a scheme with the Leicestershire Yeomanry.	
	22nd		Lieut. Hon. M. H. PALMER went on 10 days leave to England.	
	25th		2/Lieut. CHAPPLE went on 10 days leave to England.	
			Nos 2.3.4.6.&6 subsections took part in a scheme with the 2nd Life Guards and Leicestershire Yeomanry. Lieut. HAWTHORN went on 10 days leave to England.	
			The following N.C.Os were confirmed in their rank. 2801. A/Sgt/M Ross. 2774. A/Cpl. CARTER. 2800 A/Shoeing M. Spurrier. 2779. A/Cpl./M. MARTEN. confirmed as Shoeing Sgt. 9th. 2779 A/Cpl. CARTER.	
	28th		Major. CHOMLEY and Lieut. TRAFFORD went on 10 days leave to England.	
	29th		A/C.S.M. OLIVER went on a course to CAMIERS.	

WAR DIARY
INTELLIGENCE SUMMARY
(Erase heading not required.)

Army Form C. 2118.

Page I 7 M.G. Sqdn Vol 21

Instructions regarding War Diaries and Intelligence Summaries are contained in F.S. Regs., Part II. and the Staff Manual respectively. Title pages will be prepared in manuscript.

Place	Date	Hour	Summary of Events and Information	Remarks and references to Appendices
BOURS	Oct. 1917 3rd		Ruperland TERROT (utiliphile) left to be attached to American Army.	
	7th		2/Lt C. HAWTHORN from English leave. Lt N.S. ROUSE proceeded to England to take over command of recruit Squadron at Uckfield.	
	10th		Squadron marched to QUENTIN (CALONNE-SUR-LYS)	
	11th		Major G.G.F. CHOMLEY & 2/Lt TRAFFORD R.H.G.	
	13th		1st L. HARRINGTON arrived from England and attached to No. 3 S/section.	
	18th		1st L. HARRINGTON and 25 O.Rs. on detached duty to build huts in TERINS area.	
	19th		Squadron moved from QUENTIN to ROEBECQ.	
	22nd		Squadron marched to HESTRUS	
	23rd		" " SERICOURT & SIBBIVILLE.	
	24th		" " DOMQUEOR & LE TROUY. (3 S/sections).	
	27th		30 O.Rs. as reinforcements to the mounted party.	

Weyland Capt
for O.C. 7 M.G. Squadron

Army Form C. 2118.

7th Machine Gun Squadron

Vol 21

WAR DIARY
INTELLIGENCE SUMMARY
(Erase heading not required.)

Place	Date	Hour	Summary of Events and Information	Remarks and references to Appendices
DOMQUEUR	1917 Nov. 1st–16th		Squadron in DOMQUEUR & PLOUY.	
ST. GRATIEN	17th		Squadron marched to St GRATIEN. Lt CHAPPLE & 2/Lt HARRINGTON with disbursement.	
			Party by lorries to TROYART.	
PROYART.	18th		Sqdn marched to TROYART, by night.	
	19–22		Sqdn remained 'standing-to' at TROYART.	
BEAUCOURT	23rd		Sqdn marched to BEAUCOURT sur L'HALLUE where squadron remained standing-to off and on.	
	30th		Orders received for Sqdn dismounted party to proceed by lorries at 6.30 a.m. to BERNES. [MAJOR CHOMLEY, Lts PHILIPSON, PELHAM, ENGLISH, HARRINGTON, TRAFFORD and 2/Lt HARRINGTON and 97 ORs] only 8 Guns were taken with dismounted party.	

Sheppard Captain
7th M. Gun Squadron

[stamp: MACHINE GUN SQUADRON — CAVALRY BRIGADE]

WAR DIARY

Army Form C. 2118.

page. 1.
7 M.G. Sqdn
Vol 23

INTELLIGENCE SUMMARY.
(Erase heading not required.)

November 1916

Place	Date	Hour	Summary of Events and Information	Remarks and references to Appendices
BEAUCOURT SUR L'HALLUE	Dec 1st		French party left billets. 6 officers, 97 O.Rs.	
			The officers were Major J. S. L. CHOLMLEY, ~~Lt.~~	
			Lt. T. PHILIPSON. Lt. HON. M. PELHAM. L/Cpl. ENGLISH. 2/Lt. E. LEV.	
			TRAFFORD. 2/Lt. L. HARRINGTON.	
			3409 Tr. WHITEHEAD killed in action.	
			CAPT. T. PHILIPSON evacuated sick to England.	
			2/Lt. HARRISON joined the Squadron from the base.	
TRENCHES	Dec 10		2/Lt. LE.P. BERESFORD PEIRS rejoined the Squadron from the base.	
	Dec 8		CAPT. C.O.D. LEYLAND left for by land on 14 days special leave.	
	Dec 22		The Squadron moved from BEAUCOURT SUR L'HALLUE to BERNEUIL.	
BERNEUIL	"		H.Q. & 2 Sections were billeted at BERNEUIL	
			2/ Section at ST HILAIRE	
			1/ Section at LANCHES	
			1/ Section at GORGES	

WAR DIARY

Instructions regarding War Diaries and Intelligence Summaries are contained in F.S. Regs, Part II. and the Staff Manual respectively. Title pages will be prepared in manuscript.

INTELLIGENCE SUMMARY. January 1918.
(Erase heading not required.)

Page 1. 7 M.G. Sqdn
Army Form C. 2118.

Place	Date	Hour	Summary of Events and Information	Remarks and references to Appendices
BERNEUIL	Jan 1918 5		2/Lt B Harrison evacuated to hospital from french party.	
	7		Lieut Purvis RHG wounded.	
	15		Major G.G.F. CHOMLEY appointed M.G.O. to towards Division	
	15		French party under command of Lt TREFUSIS rejoin Squadron in base.	
			Capt. C.D. Copland appointed to command 7 M.G.S.	
	21		absorbed 2nd in command 7 M.G.S.	
	27		Lt Harrison returned from hospital	
	30		Lt Brighton M.G. joining Squadron from Wittles as reinforcement	
	31		Squadron reached rail head BERNEUIL to BREILLY	
			" " BREILLY to BAIZIEUX	
			Lt Trefusis went on 14 days leave England.	

Army Form C. 2118.

WAR DIARY
INTELLIGENCE SUMMARY.
(Erase heading not required.)

Instructions regarding War Diaries and Intelligence Summaries are contained in F. S. Regs, Part II. and the Staff Manual respectively. Title pages will be prepared in manuscript.

7th M.G. Squadron February 1918

Page 1

Place	Date	Hour	Summary of Events and Information	Remarks and references to Appendices
W3CST.	Feb 1918 1st		The Squadron marched from BAYONVILLERS to TREFCON	
	8th		Lts. CHAPPLE BROUGHTON + HARRISON and 43 O.R's proceeded with Squad to trenches.	
	13th		16 O.R's proceeded to 3 Cav. Div. Pioneer Regt.	
	25th		Lts. ENGLISH BERESFORD-PEIRSE + HARRINGTON relieved the above 3 officers.	
	28th		2 O.R.'s reinforcement received from Base.	

B Stafford
M.G. Squadron
for O.C. 7th M.G. Squadron

Army Form C. 2118.

WAR DIARY
INTELLIGENCE SUMMARY
(Erase heading not required.)

Page 1.

Place	Date	Hour	Summary of Events and Information	Remarks and references to Appendices
	March 1918.			
TREFCON	3rd – 9th		Squadron branch party consisting of 3 officers and 43 ORs relieved. Squadron remained at TREFCON. (9th – 27 horses handed over to munitions convoy (New York)	
WIENCOURT.	10th		Squadron moved from TREFCON to WIENCOURT.	
BRIQUEMESNIL	11th		" " WIENCOURT to BRIQUEMESNIL.	
FONTAINE	12th		" " BRIQUEMESNIL to FONTAINE.	
EPAGNE.	13th		" " FONTAINE to EPAGNE.	
"	13th to 25th		Squadron in billets at EPAGNE. disposal of horses in accordance with Nowell & Baily Demobilisation Scheme. 2 parties proceeded to MARSEILLES and DIEPPE respectively on	
"	22nd/23rd		– leaving only Transport Horses + the 35 Riding horses retained in accordance with instructions.	
ARRAS.	25th		Squadron moved in 'buses from EPAGNE to FAUBERG ST SAUVEUR ARRAS. Transport by road to FIENVILLERS	
FAUBERG ST SAUVEUR	27th		Surplus riding horses despatched with party of 11 men to ROYAL HORSE GUARDS. Squadron in trenches.	
			Transport at WARLUS.	
	29th		Following Battle Casualties:– 30411. Dpr WINTER. G. 1st RHGuards. Killed.	
			29777. " HUTCHINSON J. 2nd LHGuards. Killed	
			2806 bis " of Horse HALL E. 1st LHGuards. Wounded	
			1457. " " SMITH. A. RHGuards. Wounded.	
			16090/SqR " OWEN. R. RHGuards. Wounded	
			1572. SqR " KETTLE. J. RHGuards. Wounded	
			2916. " " SHARP. H. 3rd LHGuards. Wounded.	

7th Cav.Bde.
3rd Cav.Div.

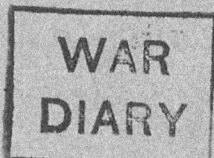

7th MACHINE GUN SQUADRON.

A P R I L

(1st to 14th)

1 9 1 8

Officer i/c Records,
Cavalry Records
Base.

Herewith War Diary
of 7th Machine Gun
Squadron from
March 1st to April 14th.
On latter date the
personnel of 7th M.G. Sqdrn
was split up among the
3 Household Cavalry
Regiments in accordance
with Demobilisation
Instructions received from
G.H.Q.

[signature] Capt.
O/C 7th M.G. Squadron.

3 MAY 1919

Army Form C. 2118.

Page 11. 7 M.G. Squadron
7.M.G.7

WAR DIARY
or
INTELLIGENCE SUMMARY.

(Erase heading not required.)

Instructions regarding War Diaries and Intelligence Summaries are contained in F. S. Regs., Part II. and the Staff Manual respectively. Title pages will be prepared in manuscript.

Place	Date	Hour	Summary of Events and Information	Remarks and references to Appendices
	April 1918		On 2nd March 2 Squadron under Major Chandos-Pole attacked the Holman & 1st Strong and also 3 Squadron under Lieut Hon ms Wm lee	Closed
WAGNONLIEU	1st		Transport moved from WARLUS to WAGNONLIEU 3 Squadron Lewis gun party reported	
	1st to 11th		Squadron remained at WAGNONLIEU.	
RAMECOURT	12th		Squadron moved by bus from WAGNONLIEU to RAMECOURT. Transport by road.	
CONTES	13th		" " " " RAMECOURT to CONTES.	
ETAPLES	14th		" " " " CONTES to ETAPLES.	
			On 14th that immediately on arrival at ETAPLES the officers and men of 7th Machine Gun Squadron (composed of 1st LIFE GUARDS, 2nd LIFE GUARDS & ROYAL HORSE GUARDS) rejoined their respective Regiments, in accordance with Demobilisation Scheme.	

A.J. Howell
Major.

O/C. 7th Machine Gun Squadron

Army Form C. 2118

WAR DIARY
INTELLIGENCE SUMMARY
(Erase heading not required.)

7TH MACHINE GUN SQUADRON

MAY 1918

Place	1918 Date May	Hour	Summary of Events and Information	Remarks and references to Appendices
FIEFS	1		The Brigade was in reserve to XI Corps and was on 3½ hours' notice.	
"	2		The Squadron was inspected by the Brigadier (Brig. Gen. A. BURT, DSO).	4-5-18. Notification received that name of Squadron was changed to "7TH M.G. Squadron
"	4		The Division was ordered to move into 4th Army area; the Brigade marched by EPS & WAVRANS, the Squadron billeting at LINZEUX.	
LINZEUX	5		March continued Southwards by FILLIEVRES - HARAVESNES - WAVANS, the Squadron billeting at MAIZICOURT.	
MAIZICOURT	6		March continued S.E., by BERNAVILLE - CANDAS & HÉRISSART, to CONTAY. The Div. was now in reserve to III Corps (4th Army), in expectation of enemy offensive.	
CONTAY	7 8 9		The Division was on 1½ hours' notice. Officers of the Squadron reconnoitred the various reserve French lines in III Corps front between SENLIS, HENENCOURT & BAISIEUX.	
"	10 11		The Brigade stood to at ½ hour notice from 5 to 8 a.m., being "duty brigade"; each brigade during this 2 days out of 3.	
"	12		Brigade on 1½ hrs' notice.	
"	13 14		Brigade on ½ hr's notice 5 a.m. — 8 a.m.; then 1½ hours	
"	17		The Division (less Can. Cav. Bde) moved West, the Brigade marching by VILLERS BOCAGE & VIGNACOURT to ST. OUEN, all units being in camp S.W. of the town.	
ST. OUEN	19		Presentation of medal ribbons by the Corps Commander.	
"	20		The Squadron was inspected by the Brigade Commander (Lt. Col. E. PATERSON, DSO)	
"	21 22 23		Cavalry Training; this included field firing & mounted work. A & B Sections also worked with 2 m.g. killings & 7th D.Gs respectively.	

(continued)

WAR DIARY or INTELLIGENCE SUMMARY

Army Form C. 2118

(2.) MAY 1918

7TH M.G. SQUADRON

Place	Date 1918 May	Hour	Summary of Events and Information	Remarks and references to Appendices
ST. OUEN	24	-	The Brigade relieved the Canadian Cav Bde as III Corps reserve in the forward area, marching by VIGNACOURT – VILLERS BOCAGE & MOLLIENS-AU-BOIS to BEHENCOURT, the Squadron having its H.Q. in MONTIGNY. The Brigade was now on 1¾ hrs' notice.	
MONTIGNY	25 26 27 28 29 30	-	A certain amount of training was done and all horses were practised over jumps, including pack horses.	
"	31	-	The Brigade was relieved in the forward area by 6th Cav. Bde., and moved West, marching by COISY & BERTANGLES to BELLOY-SUR-SOMME; the Squadron camped in the marshes S. of the village.	
BELLOY-SUR-SOMME	-			

T. Preston
CAPTAIN
COMMANDING 7th MACHINE GUN SQUADRON

Army Form C. 2118

WAR DIARY.

JUNE 1918

INTELLIGENCE SUMMARY

(Erase heading not required.)

7TH MACHINE GUN SQUADRON

Instructions regarding War Diaries and Intelligence Summaries are contained in F.S. Regs., Part II. and the Staff Manual respectively. Title Pages will be prepared in manuscript.

Place	Date 1918 June	Hour	Summary of Events and Information	Remarks and references to Appendices
BELLOY-SUR-SOMME	1 to 13		The Squadron carried out cavalry training, including pole fighting and jumping horses. The Division was still administered by III Corps.	
"	14	—	The Bde. relieved 6th Cav. Bde. in forward area marching via BERTANGLES & VILLERS BOCAGE; the Squadron occupied its former camp at MONTIGNY.	
MONTIGNY	15–18		Officers reconnoitred the trench systems in FRANVILLERS – BAISIEUX – WARLOY area	
"	19	12.30 pm –6 pm	MONTIGNY & BEHENCOURT shelled by H.V. gun; the Squadron had 7 horse casualties & 1 man slightly wounded.	
"	22		The Bde. was relieved by Canadian Cav. Bde. and marched via COISY – BERTANGLES & VAUX to ST. OUEN.	
ST. OUEN	23–30		Cavalry training & staff rides.	

T. Preston Major
COMMANDING 7th MACHINE GUN SQUADRON

Army Form C. 2118

July 1918
7 M.G. Squad
WR 30

WAR DIARY
INTELLIGENCE SUMMARY
(Erase heading not required.)

Place	Date	Hour	Summary of Events and Information	Remarks and references to Appendices
St Ouen.	July 1. 31.		The Squadron carried out Cavalry training Tuesdays &c during this period.	

Murray Capt
COMMANDING 7TH MACHINE GUN SQUADRON

WAR DIARY or INTELLIGENCE SUMMARY

AUGUST 1918 7 M.G. Sqdn

Place	Date	Hour	Summary of Events and Information	Remarks and references to Appendices
ST OUEN	4/8	10 pm	Major PRESTON, M.C. went on Paris leave yesterday. The Squadron carried on training.	
ST OUEN	5/8			
BOURDON	6/7	11 pm	Marched to BOURDON	
	7/8	9 pm	Marched to MONTIÈRES (AMIENS)	
	8/8	2, 4 am 5	Assembly Point on road between BOVES and GUYSY. 3rd Cav. Bde marched to Subdivision. Marched with 7 D.G. and 17 L. marched thro' T.R. Ris regiments and attack commenced 4.20 a.m. and out-sections 2, 4 Y.S. moved forward in reserve. Capt N. GRAY & 3rd in Command acting O.C. was killed 1, 3 & 6 sub-sections moved forward. All the Squadron was then ordered to CAYEUX WOOD. During the Sqdn's move near CAYEUX WOOD — remained on duty but to-day's moving meant 2 Bde were casualties. This action 1 OR casualty — remained on duty but to-day's moving meant 3 on the morning Capt GRAY was killed & valley between CAYEUX and CAIX and sub-section 2, 4 and 6 went into Lieut N.G. WAKEFIELD assumed command when Capt GRAY was killed relieved by infantry during the night. Brigade bivouaced opp. 2 CAYEUX. Moved between into reserve during early morning. Brigade bivouaced opp. 2 CAYEUX.	
		5 am	Squadron went up west YRELY to relieve 3rd Cavalry Division. The sub-sections & H.Q. all went that road.	
	9/8		that remained & sub 1, 3 + 5 still in reserve.	
	10	3 pm	Moved with the Brigade to just W of FOLIES.	
	11/8	10 am	No 3 sub-section relieved No 14 with No 7 D.G.	
		4 pm	Lieut R.S. HYAMS and 2nd Lt G.E. BOOTH joined squadron	
		5.30 pm	Brigade orders to move back and we went via BOVES to point just west of DOM MARTIN arriving.	
	12		Remained here resting. Major PRESTON, M.C. rejoined about 5 pm.	
	2/8 13/8		Major PRESTON M.C. went to hospital. Relieved by Lt Col. PATTERSON, 6 Dub. Regt brigadier of brigade. Lt. B.B. GRIFFIN rejoined from Cavalry Corps School. Supplied and assumed command.	

1875 Wt. W593/826 1,000,000 4/15 J.B.C. & A. A.D.S.S./Forms/C.2118.

WAR DIARY
or
INTELLIGENCE SUMMARY

Army Form C. 2118

Place	Date	Hour	Summary of Events and Information	Remarks and references to Appendices
W.OF DOMMARTIN	15th	8·15 p.m.	Brigade moved and marched during night to ST OUEN via BOVES, AMIENS, LONGPRÉ arriving about 3 a.m.	
ST. OUEN	16th		Refitting, training, reinforcements and remounts	
	17th			
	18th			
	19th		Lieut. W. G. GREENSTREET, M.C. rejoined from leave U.K.	
	20th			
	21st		Stood to on 2½ hours notice to move.	
	22nd			
	23rd			
	24th			
LE BOISLE	25th	9pm	Brigade marched to LE BOISLE area	
CANCHY	26th	6pm	" " " CANCHY area	
	27th	10am	Stood to on ½ hour notice to move, later 2½ hrs no. later 2.P.W. STROUD joined the Squadron	
	28th		On 2½ hours notice to move	
	29th			
	30th		Capt. B.S. ROBINSON joined Squadron as 2nd in Command; proceeded on command until arrival of C.O.	
	31st		On 5½ hours notice to move	

B.S. Robinson   Capt.

WAR DIARY
or
INTELLIGENCE SUMMARY
(Erase heading not required.)

SEPTEMBER 1918 Army Form C. 2118

7TH MACHINE GUN SQUADRON

Vol 32

Place	Date 1918 Sept	Hour	Summary of Events and Information	Remarks and references to Appendices
FILLIÈVRES	6	-	Major T. PRESTON, MC, rejoined from hospital and resumed command of the Squadron.	
	10		The Squadron moved to fresh billets at ROUGEFAY	
ROUGEFAY	12		"B" Section was moved to BUIRE-AU-BOIS, thus enabling all horses to be under cover.	
"	16		The Brigade moved north to the TERNOISE valley for manoeuvres, the Squadron billeting in BLINGEL Camp.	
BLINGEL	17		Cavalry Corps Manoeuvres, under the Commander in Chief, took place finishing 3 pm at AUXI-LE-CHATEAU where a Conference was held. The Division did not actually get in action. At the end of the day the Squadron billeted at HEUZECOURT.	
HEUZECOURT	18		The Squadron returned to its former billets at ROUGEPAY & BUIRE-AU-BOIS.	
ROUGEFAY	19		Billeting areas were adjusted and the Squadron moved to GALAMETZ.	
GALAMETZ	25		In connection with operations in the CAMBRAI – ST QUENTIN front the Division marched South-Eastwards. The Brigade moved (at night) by CONCHY-SUR-CANCHE, BONNIÈRES & DOULLENS, the Squadron billeting at TERRAMESNIL	
TERRAMES-NIL	26		March continued by LOUVENCOURT & FORCEVILLE to AVELUY. (arr. 2 am)	
AVELUY	27		March continued by ALBERT & MARICOURT to HEM, where the Bde. halted the following day (28th)	
HEM	28		On 29th there were no orders to move	
	29	4 pm	the Division marched by PÉRONNE, DOINGT & POEUILLY the Bde. being at VERMAND. "B" Echelon was Divisionalised at CURLU.	
VERMAND	30		The Division was 3 hours on the move.	

T Preston
MAJOR
COMMANDING 7TH MACHINE GUN SQUADRON

Army Form C. 2118

WAR DIARY (1) OCTOBER 1918
INTELLIGENCE SUMMARY
(Erase heading not required.)

7TH MACHINE GUN SQUADRON Vol 3

Instructions regarding War Diaries and Intelligence Summaries are contained in F.S. Regs, Part II. and the Staff Manual respectively. Title Pages will be prepared in manuscript.

Place	Date 1918 Oct	Hour	Summary of Events and Information	Remarks and references to Appendices
VERMAND	1		The Brigade was on 1 hour's notice to move.	
"	2	08.45	The Bde. moved from VERMAND to W. of BELLENGLISE, but owing to enemy	
"		10.50	counter attack at RAMICOURT, cavalry were ordered back, the Bde returning to VERMAND.	
"	3	10.45	The Division moved to assembly area W. of BELLENGLISE. The Squadron was divided as follows:- N° 1 Subsection (2/Lr. C.P.W. STROUD) to 6th Drd; " 3 " (Lieut. F.B. TAYLOR) to 7th D. Gds " 5 " (Lieut. C.L. SNODGRASS) to 17th L/s 2 Bde. { " 2 " (Lieut. W.G. WAKEFIELD MC) reserve { " 4 " (Lieut. R.G. FAITHFULL) { " 6 " (Lieut. W. GREENSTREET MC)	
BELLENGLISE	"	16.00	The Bde. followed 6th Cav. Bde. over ST. QUENTIN Canal & moved into	
MAGNY-LA-FOSSE	"		valley S.W. of MAGNY-LA-FOSSE, but at 19.00 the Division was	
"	"	19.00	ordered back to VERMAND area, the Squadron billeting at N.E. end of VERMAND village.	
VERMAND	4		The Bde. was on 3½ hours' notice.	
"	7		Lieut R.S. HYAMS left the Squadron for Cav. Corps Reinforcement Camp.	
"	8		Attack by III & IV British Armies, 2nd American Corps, & I French Army	
JONCOURT		08.00	The Bde. moved to assembly area S. of JONCOURT arriving 08.00. The Squadron was divided as on Oct 3rd. Later in the morning the Bde. moved forward to valley at GENEVE, just S. of LE CATEAU Roman road.	

WAR DIARY (2) OCTOBER 1918

INTELLIGENCE SUMMARY

7TH M.G. SQUADRON

Army Form C. 2118.

Place	Date 1918 Oct	Hour	Summary of Events and Information	Remarks and references to Appendices
GENEVE	8	17.00	Owing to 1st Cav. Div failing to get very far, 3rd Cav. Div was ordered back; the Bde moved to ETRICOURT, the squadron joining up and billeting S. of NAUROY	
ETRICOURT	9	04.00	Attack continued. The Bde moved from ETRICOURT to assembly area in same valley at GENEVE, where the squadron detailed Subsections 1, 3, & 5 to 6th Dns, 7th D.G's and 17th Lrs as before.	
GENEVE		06.00	The Division were now leading Div'n; the Bde sent 17th Lrs and 6th Dns (with Subsections 5 and 1, 7th M.G.S) to forward positions near VAUX-LE-PRETRE chateau. Later, the Division sent 6th & Canadian Bdes forward and 7th Cav Bde was in reserve.	
		10.00	moving past SERAIN to near MARETZ	
MARETZ		15.00	About 15.00, following on successful advance by Canadian & 6th Cav. Bdes, 7th Cav Bde moved forward by HONNECHY & MAUROIS to N.W. of REUMONT, where Canadian Bde. had established a line. The 3 Subsec ※	
REUMONT		17.00	(Lt. F.B.TAYLOR) with a squadron of 7th D.G's passed the night in REUMONT; 1 & 1 Subsec (2 Lt. C.P.STROUD) with 6th Dns. The remaining 4 Subsections concentrated with the Brigade. In the night 9th/10th	
	10	05.15	6th Dns were detailed to send a reconnoitring squadron to LE CATEAU & were allotted 2 & 2 subsec (Lt. W.G. WAKEFIELD MC). In addition	
			※ About 17.00, this subsec got some shooting at enemy infantry digging themselves in E. of REUMONT. About 4 MGs were fired at 700+ with good effect	

WAR DIARY (3)
INTELLIGENCE SUMMARY
7TH M.G. SQUADRON
OCTOBER 1918

Army Form C. 2118.

Place	Date 1918 Oct	Hour	Summary of Events and Information	Remarks and references to Appendices
REUMONT	10		to 2/1 Subsec. At the same time, 2.0. 4 Subsec. (Lt. R.G. FAITHFULL) and	
		06:30	No. 6 Subsec (2/Lt. W. GREENSTREET) were allotted to 7th D.G's advanced squadron which reconnoitred NEUVILLY. All four subsections got	
		08:00	a little long-range firing (2000–2500 x) and 192 m west of LE CATEAU and 24 at enemy Transport N. of NEUVILLY. One gun of team of No. 6 Subsec was knocked out by a shell & casualties 1 killed	
		07:30	4 wounded & horses missing 22 hour GREENSTREET was wounded. The Bde. with Subsecs. 3, 4, 5 were N.E. of TROISVILLE on CAMBRAI –	
TROISVILLE		08:30	LE CATEAU main road, but owing to shelling, withdrew later to Valley S.E. of TROISVILLE. During the morning the infantry	
		14:35	took over the line and at 14:35 the Bde. was ordered back to BERTRY where it went into billets the squadron being at the N.E. end of the village on CAUDRY road with all men under cover.	
BERTRY	11	08:30	The Bde. saddled up ready to move at 08:30. but this was cancelled later. A1 & A2 Echelons which had been divisionalised, rejoined the Squadron.	Casualties 1 Off. W. 2 O.R. K. 4 " W. 18 horses K.W.
"	12		BERTRY was shelled at intervals and the squadron had 2 horses wounded	
"	13		The Sqn moved West, the Bde. marching via CLARY, MALINCOURT & VILLERS OUTRÉAUX to HONNECOURT where it halted for the night.	

WAR DIARY (4) or INTELLIGENCE SUMMARY

(Erase heading not required.)

OCTOBER 1918 Army Form C. 2118

7TH M.G. SQUADRON

Place	Date 1918 Oct	Hour	Summary of Events and Information	Remarks and references to Appendices
HONNECOURT	14		March continued via GOUZEAUCOURT & FINS to BERTINCOURT area; the Squadron billeted at NEUVILLE - BOURJONVAL; practically all horses under cover.	
NEUVILLE - BOURJONVAL	17		Captain V.J. DAWSON joined the squadron from Cav. Corps Reinforcement Camp	
Do.	19		Inspection of "A" & "B" Echelons by O.C., A.S.C.	
	21		Training in Equitation, Judging Distance, Range Taking, Gun Classes, Field training, and study of ground by eye and with field glasses. Shooting on a 25 yds Range. During this period the Squadron took part in 3 Tactical Schemes in conjunction with the rest of the Brigade. Lieut. G.G. Roberts joined from Base, and Captain Robinson returned from leave, 25th. Lieut. Hyams rejoined from Cavalry Reinforcement Camp, 27th. Major V.J. DAWSON left for U.K. on duty, Major V.J. DAWSON assuming Command 27th	
	31		During the month 37 O.Ranks came as Reinforcements, and 20 horses were taken onto the strength.	

WAR DIARY
or
INTELLIGENCE SUMMARY

Army Form C. 2118

No. 1. NOVEMBER 1918.

7th MACHINE GUN SQUADRON.

JR 34

Place	Date	Hour	Summary of Events and Information	Remarks and references to Appendices
NUYELLE	1-5		Training:— Equitation, Judging Distance, Short Range. Visual Training. On the 5th the Squadron was put on 2 hours notice.	
	6		March to SAUCHY LESTRE.	
	7		Do. to PLANQUE.	
	8		Do. to LA NUVELLE.	
TOURCOING	9		Do. to TOURCOING. No: 4 Sub section to 7th D.Gs — No: 6 Sub Sec. to 17th Lancers.	
	10		No: 3 Sub Section to 7th D.Gs — No: 5 Sub Section to 17th Lancers.	
	11		Armistice Declared. 11 o'clock.	
	16		March to FRESNES-LEZ-BUISSENAL. Nos 5 & 6 Sub sections rejoined at end of march.	
	17		March to BIEVENE. No: 4 Sub Section rejoined at commencement of march. No: 2 Sub section to 6th Cavalry Field Ambulance.	
GROOTE-HEARDING	18		Do. to GROOTE HEARDING. No: 3 Sub Section rejoined at end of march.	
			No: 6 Sub Section to 17th Lancers.	
	21		March to LES BARRQUE, HT RANSBECHE. No: 4 Sub section to 7th D.Gs.	
DONGELBERG	22-30		Do. to DONGELBERG. Sub Sections 2, 4 and 6 rejoined the Squadron.	

V.J. Dawson, Major
Commandant, 7th M.G. Squadron

WAR DIARY
or
INTELLIGENCE SUMMARY

Army Form C. 2118

7th Machine Gun Sqdn.

December 1918.

No. 1

Place	Date Dec.	Hour	Summary of Events and Information	Remarks and references to Appendices
DONGLEBERG			Dec 1st to Dec 14th inclusive.	
FUMAL	15		Left DONGLEBERG for FUMAL.	
NANDRIN	16		Left FUMAL for NANDRIN.	
	17-26		Squadron billeted in NANDRIN - TAVIER - BAUGNÉE - CHATEAU - CHATEAU - BASSINE, MEAN, MAFFE.	
MEAN.	27		Squadron moved into winter billets at BONSIN - BORLON.	

V.G.Darran Major.
COMMANDING 7TH MACHINE GUN SQUADRON

7 Mtg Squadron Army Form C. 2118

No 2

WAR DIARY
or
INTELLIGENCE SUMMARY January 1919

(Erase heading not required.)

Instructions regarding War Diaries and Intelligence Summaries are contained in F. S. Regs., Part II. and the Staff Manual respectively. Title Pages will be prepared in manuscript.

Place	Date	Hour	Summary of Events and Information	Remarks and references to Appendices
CHATEAU-BASSEUX				
MEAN	1st		January 1st to January 31st inclusive. 7 Mtg Squadron HQ stationed in MEAN MAFFE BONSIN BORZON Billets	
MAFFE			Lt. GRIFFIN left for Demobilisation	
BONSIN	21		Lt. TAYLOR left for Demobilisation	
BORZON	25		Lt. HYAMS left for Demobilisation	
area	27		Master DAWSON on Leave to UK	
	29			
	31st		Inspection of Squadron HQ and Sub-stations by two officers	

R.J. Ormsby Major
for O.C. 7 Mtg Squadron

Army Form C. 2118

WAR DIARY
or
INTELLIGENCE SUMMARY
(Erase heading not required.)

February 1919.

Vol 37

Place	Date	Hour	Summary of Events and Information	Remarks and references to Appendices
CHATEAU BASSINES. MEAN. MAFFE BONSIN. BORLON.	1st		Squadron remained in same area during whole of the month of FEBRUARY. Squadron H.Qn. at CHATEAU BASSINES. One Sub of each Sqn in MEAN. MAFFE BONSIN. BORLON. Village H.Q. Sub. Section. Horse - Board changed squadron stores	
	26.		LIEUT. CL. SNODGRASS relinquished during month of JANUARY. CAPTAIN B.S. ROBINSON 2ND. IN - COMMAND of SQUADRON) was reported in M.G.C. (CAVALRY) PART II Orders received by us about February 13th as having been due obtaining for M.G.C. BASE	
	28		MAJOR. DAWSON still on leave in U.K.	

P.J. Fairbright Lt
M.O.C 4 Sqn Squadron

Army Form C. 2118.

WAR DIARY
or
INTELLIGENCE SUMMARY.
(Erase heading not required.)

March 1919

Instructions regarding War Diaries and Intelligence Summaries are contained in F. S. Regs., Part II. and the Staff Manual respectively. Title pages will be prepared in manuscript.

Place	Date	Hour	Summary of Events and Information	Remarks and references to Appendices
BASSINES CHATEAU and area	1st		Squadron remained in this area	
"	"		Major V.J. DAWSON rejoined from leave.	
MEAN. MAFFE BONSIN. BOURLON	8		Lieut: R.G. FAITHFULL left for Demobilization	
HERMALLE sous HUY.	15		Squadron moved to HERMALLE sous HUY. Strength 4 Officers. 110 O.R.	
	18		2nd Lieut: C.W.P. STROUD left to join 9th M.G. Squadron	
	24		Lieut. R.G. BURTON left to join the 2nd Squadron	
			During the month 15 O.Rs despatched to join Army of Occupation on the Rhine	
			On 18.3.1919 Orders were received that the Squadron was to be reduced to Cadre "A".	
			134 Horses were despatched by the end of the month, for Sale in Belgium, Army of the Rhine and to England.	

V.J. Dawson
MAJOR.
COMMANDING 7TH MACHINE GUN SQUADRON

Army Form C. 2118.

7 M G Sqn

WAR DIARY
or
INTELLIGENCE SUMMARY.
(Erase heading not required.)

April 1919.

Place	Date	Hour	Summary of Events and Information	Remarks and references to Appendices
April	25		Cadre of 7th Machine Gun Squadron in Village of HERMALLE sous HUY. Loaded auto-train at ENGIS all Squadrons wagons and equipment, for despatch to B.O. at Base.	
	26		Cadre moved to new area BASSE-AWIRS, East of ENGIS.	
	30.		Strength :- Major V.J. Dawson. } 40 O.Rs 2nd Lt. G.E. Booth. }	

V.J. Dawson. MAJOR
COMMANDING 7TH MACHINE GUN SQUADRON

Army Form C. 2118

WAR DIARY
or
INTELLIGENCE SUMMARY

(Erase heading not required.)

May 1919
7th Machine Gun Squadron

Place	Date	Hour	Summary of Events and Information	Remarks and references to Appendices
BASSE-AWIRS. (Near ENGIS)	May 1		Cadre of 7th M.G. Squadron located at BASSE-AWIRS.	
	13		Train carrying Units Equipment, Wagons Etc. left for Base Ordnance Depot BEAUMARIS, with S.Q.M.S. METCALFE and 1 O.R. —	
	19		Orders received to Reduce Cadre to 1 Officer - 4 O.R. and demobilize remainder	
	20		27 O.R. } to CHARLEROI for demobilization.	
	21		1 O.R. }	
	22		Second Lieutenant G.E. BOOTH left Squadron — Granted 14 days leave in U.K. and rejoin 9th M.G.Sqdn. "Army of the Rhine".	
	23		2 O.R. returned from Ordnance Base Depot. (for U.K.)	
	27		A/S.S.M. BROOKS and A/S.Q.M.S. METCALFE - to CHARLEROI - for 3 months Recruitment furlough — Orders received that 7th M.G.Sqdn would be disbanded in this country.	
	31		Remaining in Squadron — 1 off. (Major Y.J. DAWSON) and 4 O.R.	

C.J. Dawson
Commanding 7th Machine Gun Squadron
31.5.1919

CONFIDENTIAL

Officer i/c
A.G's Office,
H.Q British Troops in France &
Flanders

———

Herewith War Diary of 7th M.G.
Squadron compiled up to June 18th
the date on which the Unit proceeded
to U.K.

R.B. Johns
Lieut.
18/6/19   3rd Cav. Div.   a/Staff Captain
              Cadre Base

Army Form C. 2118

WAR DIARY
or
INTELLIGENCE SUMMARY
(Erase heading not required.)

4th JUNE 1919 7 Machine Gun Squadron.

Place	Date JUNE.	Hour	Summary of Events and Information	Remarks and references to Appendices
BASSES-AWIRS. Near (ENGIS)	1.		Remaining party of 7th M.G. Squadron located at BASSES-AWIRS.	Ceased
	11.		MAJOR. V.J. DAWSON proceeded to U.K. for Demobilization.	
	18.		Remaining 4 O.Rs. proceeded to CHARLEROI for U.K. for Demobilization.	

Geoffrey Reid
Major
COMMANDING 7TH MACHINE GUN SQUADRON

www.ingramcontent.com/pod-product-compliance
Lightning Source LLC
Chambersburg PA
CBHW081243170426
43191CB00034B/2030